The Tale of
COSMO
The Adventurous Sheep

written by
Charis Papalas

illustrated by
Mousam Banerjee

This book is dedicated to all the
Fiery Aries around the world.

Cosmo comes from the Greek word *kosmos*, meaning "world."

Since his days as a little lamb, Cosmo had always lived high in the hills of the beautiful island of Chios. Bright sunshine lit up the clear skies, cool breezes wafted through the meadows, and there was enough grass to eat forever.

While all the other sheep in the flock were content with their lives on the island, Cosmo was not.

"But you have everything!" said Mom and Dad. "You have grass, shade, cool water to drink. We don't understand why you'd want to leave."

Cosmo only shook his little head, his horns sharp and gleaming in the afternoon sun. He was an Aries ram, which meant he was born at the vernal equinox in the spring. True to the symbolic meaning of his birth, Cosmo was full of optimism and conviction that there had to be something more out there. Something bigger. And he was determined to find it.

Filled with a burning desire for adventure, Cosmo wanted to see the world! One island was no longer enough for him.

"I'm going to explore what else is out there," he said.
"I'm going to find another island for myself!"

"Oh, he's just a foolish lamb! What does he know about
the world?" said the elder of the flock.
"He's stubborn and arrogant. Like all Aries!"

Yet, unlike the other sheep in the flock, Cosmo's Mom and Dad understood their son had to carve his own path one day.

"We love you, Cosmo, but please, be safe." They knew he was a brave boy, and the only way for their son to grow was to let him have his freedom.

And so, with his parents' blessing, Cosmo set off on his adventure. He ran down rocky hills and crossed wild forest streams until he finally made his way to the beach. This was the furthest Cosmo had ever been from home. But what was he to do now?

With no parents to guide him anymore or friends to comfort him, Cosmo felt scared. But then his gaze turned toward the sky, and his heart started beating faster. It was something he'd felt his entire life. A desire to live! To grow! To fulfill his wildest dreams!

Cosmo's eyes sparkled with hope as he knew he would be the first sheep to leave the island.

"No matter what," he whispered to himself, a tear trickling down his cheek.

Just when he thought he was all alone, Cosmo spotted an old fisherman in the distance. Most sheep were afraid of humans, but not Cosmo. He ran over and nudged the fisherman's boat with his horns.

"Oh," said the fisherman, "hello, little one. How did you get here?"

Cosmo jumped into the fisherman's boat, but the old man picked him up and put him back on the ground.

"Oh no, you don't," he said.

But Cosmo didn't give up and jumped back into the boat over and over again.

Realizing that all his attempts were in vain, the old fisherman shook his head and let out a heavy sigh. "Well... all right. I guess we're off to Samos together then."

And so the two set sail across the vast sea. Full of hope, Cosmo looked up to the bright blue sky, only to see it was slowly getting covered by gray clouds.

"Looks like it's going to rain soon, little one," said the fisherman.

Just as the fisherman finished his sentence, heavy rain started pouring from the sky, accompanied by gusts of thunder and lightning. Try as he might, the old fisherman could do nothing to row them safely to their destination, and the tiny boat got struck by lightning with a mighty thud.

Now underwater, Cosmo paddled his tiny legs, desperately trying to get to the surface. Gulping for air, he could see the shore, but the fisherman was nowhere in sight. So, Cosmo started bleating and bleating, until...

"I'm over here, little one!"

Reunited with his friend again, Cosmo nudged the old man with his head, telling him to grab his horns. With the fisherman holding onto him, the brave little ram carried on swimming all the way to the shore.

With the skies now clear, Cosmo and the fisherman made their way to Samos, its coast dwarfed by a colossal mountain.

"Where are you going, little ram?" said the fisherman as Cosmo started running inland.

But Cosmo was already heading for the mountain. It was so beautiful, and its snowy peak was so high up it kissed the sky! Cosmo couldn't believe his eyes. It was what he'd been looking for all along—a beautiful place all of his own.

But the mountain was high and steep, and menacing boulders threatened to discourage even the bravest adventurers. How would Cosmo climb it? He was only used to small hills. Aries rams never gave up, though. Cosmo remembered a song his parents used to sing to him. He started humming the tune to take his mind off the challenge ahead.

After a while and a bit further up the mountain, Cosmo spotted a few other sheep from the island. He joined them, they all introduced themselves, and the group continued their climb together. The other sheep were so happy to welcome Cosmo, they even taught him a few tricks along the way.

Even as some of his companions complained or got tired, Cosmo kept climbing. He didn't want to come last or even second. He wanted to be the first to reach the top!

With the summit getting closer and closer, Cosmo realized that this was the highest he'd ever climbed. So high, in fact, that he could almost see the island of his childhood far away in the distance. The other sheep smiled and nodded encouragingly at their new companion, urging him to press on until the entire flock disappeared high up into the clouds.

After an arduous journey, Cosmo finally made it to the top. To his surprise, even more sheep were waiting for him there. And they loved having him around. They admired him for how strong and brave he was after Cosmo shared his adventures with them.

In the end, despite all the challenges he had to face along the way, Cosmo, the Aries ram, knew that his dream had finally come true. He now had a new home, one where he felt like he truly belonged.

Traits Aries Are Best Known For:

Assertive

Competitive

Strong

Responsible

Optimistic

Loving

Independent

Stubborn

Outgoing

Adventurous

About the Author

Charis Papalas was born in Greece but raised abroad from a young age. In ancient Greece, astrologers only made horoscopes for the wealthy and for kings, the only people who could afford this luxury. Nowadays, stories and zodiacs are still of huge significance in Greek culture, and Charis's parents have diligently instilled their values throughout his childhood. Growing up surrounded by conversations revolving around people's zodiacs and moon signs, daily astrological forecasts on TV, and New-Year horoscope predictions, Charis is now hoping to impart parts of his culture to others through his endearing and captivating tales.

He currently resides in the cosmopolitan city of London, where he works in the often less exciting world of mobile media advertising. Outside of work, he spends most of his time highlighting how his friends and colleagues embody their zodiac stereotypes and has recently converted this passion into writing zodiac-centered children's stories.

When he's not writing, Charis enjoys watching anime, reading a good sci-fi book, or taking in the views of London while out rollerblading.

Charis can be found online at www.thezodiactales.com

Check www.thezodiactales.com for regular updates on the release of the second story in the Zodiac Tales series, *The Tale of Santiago, The Strong Bull.*

The second story of the Zodiac Tales, *The Tale of Santiago, The Strong Bull*, takes its readers on a new world adventure—this time to the sun-soaked countryside of Spain. Santiago, the country's most prized bull, wants to go on a treasure hunt, but everyone tells him he's going on a wild goose chase.

But, true to his star sign, the mighty Taurus, Santiago likes to do things his own way! Disciplined in his pursuit, he is early to bed and early to rise, day in, day out, leaving no stone unturned until the mysterious treasure is his.

Will he prove everyone wrong and return triumphant from his pursuits?